Coco Wyo

GIRL MOMENTS

CUTE & COMFY COLORING BOOK

This book belongs to

....

COZY COLORING COMMUNITY

Come say hi and be part of our supportive coloring community! Simply scan the QR code and let's have fun together!

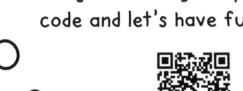

@cocowyocoloring

SHARE YOUR ARTWORKS

Let your uniqueness shine! Share your one-of-a-kind artworks with us. Don't forget to tag #cocowyo and #cocowyocoloring, we can't wait to see yours!

⟡ CUTE PATTERNS ⟡

Heart →

Plaid →

Flower ←

← Bow

Leaf ←

A blank sheet of paper

TEST COLOR PAGE

Coco Wyo x Penguin Random House

Special Edition

COZY CHRISTMAS

CocoWyo ♥ Hope you enjoy this coloring page

Made in the USA
Columbia, SC
05 December 2024

48484312R00050